Dra

illustrated by
Nick Schon
Chiara Pasqualotto
Andy Elkerton

CONTENTS

George and the Dragon ------------------------------- 3
Tchang and the Pearl Dragon -------------------- 25
The Bamburgh Dragon ------------------------------- 47

OXFORD
UNIVERSITY PRESS

Dear Reader,

Imagine a dragon. Most people think of a fire-breathing creature, covered in scales with wings, claws and a long tail.

Now, how do you think dragons usually behave? Your answer will depend on where you live. In Western countries, such as the United Kingdom, most dragons are fierce monsters that will eat you as soon as catch sight of you. In Eastern countries, such as China, dragons are thought of as wise and good.

In the following stories, you'll meet both kinds of dragon. I hope you enjoy them all!

Andy Blackford

George and the Dragon

A legend from Libya, North Africa

Chapter 1

It was midday. The marketplace should have been ringing with the cries of traders. It should have been buzzing with the chatter of women. Instead it was silent and deserted.

The sun beat down on heaps of fruit, piles of pots and brightly-coloured silks. The people peered anxiously from behind the shutters of their homes.

Then the silence was torn by a savage roar. The
air was filled with the stench of burning. Into
the market square lumbered a terrible dragon.
Its body was covered in blue-green scales. Its
bloodshot eyes glowed like coals. Its claws, long
and sharp as daggers, struck sparks from the
cobblestones. Foul smoke poured from its nostrils.

'Hello-o-o, people!' it roared. 'It's twelve o'clock, and twelve o'clock is maiden time. But wait – I see no maiden! Well, I'm afraid it won't do. It won't do at all!'

A ball of fire burst from its jaws and ballooned into the blue sky.

'I was looking forward to a take-away, but I suppose a home delivery will have to do. Deliver a maiden to my lair by noon, seven days from today. Otherwise I'll turn this town to rubble and everyone in it to crisps!'

The monster turned and dragged its hideous bulk back along the stony track towards its cave.

Slowly, the people came out from their houses and gathered in the square.

'Well, you heard the dragon,' said the Mayor. 'We'd better take him a maiden or we're all doomed!'

'That's all very well,' the cobbler pointed out, 'but we've run out of maidens.'

The Mayor groaned. 'Oh, come along! Surely there must be one or two around somewhere? Think!'

High upon a crag stood the Sultan's castle. His daughter, the Princess Sabra, sat by her window and listened to the people. A single tear rolled down her cheek.

Then she stood up and marched to her mother's room. 'I must give myself up to the dragon or else he will destroy the town and everyone in it!'

'Don't be silly, dear,' replied the Sultana. 'You're a princess. One of the peasant girls will have to go.'

'There aren't any left,' said Sabra. 'The dragon has eaten them all. Besides, as a princess, it is my duty to be brave and set a good example.'

Her mother shook her head. 'Your father will never agree to it.'

The Sultan was terribly upset by the idea of losing his beloved daughter. He knew that without a miracle, Sabra would die. 'Still,' he said, 'I'll send out a plea for help. You never know, something might turn up.'

He wrote a message and attached it to the leg of his best falcon. 'Fly like the wind, bird!' he commanded.

Chapter 2

Meanwhile, in England, a young knight was pacing up and down while his mother did her embroidery. 'I'm bored,' he muttered. His mother didn't look up. 'Bored, bored, *bored*,' he repeated. Still she ignored him. *'Bored, bored, bored, BORED, BORED ...'*

She slammed down her sewing. 'George! What is the matter with you?'

'Nothing!' he snapped. 'Except I haven't slain anything for weeks!'

His mother said, 'You slew that huge serpent, when was it, last Tuesday?'

'The serpent was a pushover,' said George. 'When was the last time I saved a beautiful maiden from certain death?'

'I don't know, dear, I don't keep count.'

'Well, I'll tell you, Mother. It was last April. April! And you might not keep count, but the other knights do. I'm a laughing stock!'

They were interrupted by a sharp tapping sound at the window. Perched on the sill was a handsome falcon. The bird stepped inside and held out its leg. George unfurled the message:

Come at once. Dragon trouble, maiden in distress, etc.
Yours sincerely,
The Sultan of Libya.

P.S. Wear armour.
P.P.S. Recommend long spear.
P.P.P.S. Better bring sword, too.

'Excellent!' cried the delighted George. 'That's more like it! A monster to slay *AND* a maiden to rescue!' Then he twirled his poor mother around until she was quite dizzy. Soon he was galloping off towards the harbour on Rover, his trusty steed.

'Do be careful, dear!' his mother called after him. 'Dragons can be tricky!'

'Don't worry, Mum,' George replied cheerily. 'This spear's got a ten-year guarantee!'

So, following the Sultan's falcon, George set off on the long journey to Africa.

Chapter 3

George and Rover climbed snow-capped
mountains. They swam across rushing rivers.
They toiled over trackless deserts.

Finally, they arrived at the Sultan's palace.
George rang the bell but nobody answered.
He pushed open the door. 'Hullo?' he called.
'Anybody home? Bold knight here, come to
sort out dragon trouble, rescue maiden, etc.!'

He clanked up the stairs in his heavy armour. The sound of pitiful weeping drew him to a room where he found the Sultana.

'There, there!' he said, offering her his hankie. 'Whatever's wrong, I'm sure I can help. I'm a knight in shining armour!' Then he caught sight of himself in a mirror. 'Well, armour, at any rate.'

'It's my daughter,' the Sultana sobbed. 'She's gone to give herself up to a dragon!'

'Yikes!' cried George. 'There's not a moment to lose!' He clattered back downstairs. 'Lead the way, bird!' he ordered the falcon. Soon he was galloping off towards the mountain where the dragon lived.

It was a slow, sad procession that wound its way towards the dragon's lair. There was a great deal of weeping and a fair bit of wailing. In his carriage, the Sultan beat his chest and tore at his beard in misery.

Only the Princess Sabra held her head high as she walked proud and silent at the head of the procession.

Before them loomed the great, black mountain with its sinister cave. A mighty roar echoed from deep within the rock.

The people shuddered and cried out in terror. But Sabra continued her dignified walk towards her horrible fate.

As she reached the mouth of the cave, she was almost knocked off her feet by a blast of hot, stinking smoke.

'Aha!' growled the dragon. 'Better late than never, I suppose. But why the parade? I didn't order a starter!'

The people scattered, screaming, and the
dragon roared with laughter. His mirth was
cut short by a clatter of hooves and a rattle of
armour. 'Oh dear,' sneered the dragon, 'What
have we here? A sardine tin with legs?'

'Whoah!' cried George. 'Princess! Get
back to the palace! RUN!'

Sabra looked surprised. 'And just who
are you?'

'Never mind that now!' George snapped.
'Go on home while I deal with the worm.'

'Worm?' shrieked the dragon. 'WORM?'
It charged at George lashing its tail with its
wicked barbs.

George bent his head, raised his spear,
dug his spurs into Rover's sides and lurched
forward at the dragon. The spear caught the
dragon square on its chest – and snapped
in two.

'Bother!' exclaimed George. 'I shall jolly well
demand my money back!'

The dragon bore down upon him, eyes
blazing and flames spurting from its nostrils.
Princess Sabra shouted, 'Get under the tree!'

By the mouth of the cave there grew a tree, its boughs groaning with oranges. George spurred Rover under its shade and, to his amazement, the dragon didn't follow them. It just paced angrily up and down, growling and spitting fire.

'Well,' George remarked, 'Thank heavens for magic orange trees!' Then he jumped down from Rover, drew his sword and raced towards the dragon. The monster snarled and belched a great jet of fire.

Now George was so close to the dragon that he almost choked on its foul, scorching breath. His eyes were watering so much, he could barely see. Yet he drew back his arm and aimed his sword at a soft spot just under its wing. The tip of the blade slipped between the dragon's scales and sliced into its side.

With a howl of rage, the dragon raised its
terrible claw to strike. George closed his eyes
and prayed. Then there was an awful groan and
a crash that shook the ground.

George opened his eyes to see the beast
collapsed in a heap. A wisp of smoke rose from
its open jaws.

A red glow still burned in its eyes – until
George strode up and with one terrible blow,
cut off its head.

***

Back at the palace, the grateful Sultan threw a magnificent banquet for George and Rover.

Next morning, George clambered onto the trusty Rover and bade farewell to Princess Sabra. She wiped away a tear. 'Must you leave so soon?'

'Afraid so,' replied George. 'You know how it is – maidens to slay, dragons to save, etc.!'

'Wrong way round!' whispered Rover.

'Whatever!' cried George, and with a cheery wave, he galloped off towards England and home.

Tchang and the Pearl Dragon

A myth from China

Chapter 1

A boy sat on the shore of a deep, blue lake in old China. He had been sitting there with his fishing rod since sunrise but he hadn't caught a single fish. Wearily, he packed away his rod and trudged back to the little cottage where he lived.

Now it so happened
that a great, green water
dragon was passing by. It was on
its way home to a far-off river.
The dragon had tiny wings and
in its forehead was a huge pearl.
The pearl flashed brightly in the
sun – so brightly that the boy
was dazzled and could not even
see the dragon. He thought it
was just the sun in his eyes.

The boy looked so unhappy
that the dragon felt sorry for
him. He decided to follow
the boy.

His mother was working in the garden, which was just a patch of dried-up dirt. She came running to greet him. 'Well? What did you catch?'

He couldn't meet her eye. 'Nothing, mother,' he replied miserably.

She slumped down on a log with her face in her hands. 'Oh, what are we going to do? This land is dried up and dead. We don't have a thing to eat.'

The boy was called Tchang. He and his mother slaved all day, trying to scrape together enough to stay alive. But things were getting worse and worse. There were no longer any fish in the lake and very little grew in the barren soil.

The dragon overheard Tchang talking with his mother. Its heart went out to them. That night, when Tchang's mother was sleeping, the dragon gently touched her brow with the tip of his magic wing.

Next morning, Tchang's mother knew just what to do. 'You must go and visit the Great Wizard of the West,' she told Tchang. 'Ask him why we are so very, very poor when we work so very, very hard.'

So Tchang kissed his mother goodbye and set out for the West. He carried only a few scraps of bread wrapped up in a handkerchief.

Chapter 2

For forty-nine days Tchang trudged across deserts and over mountains until he came to a dark forest. His bread had run out long ago and he was so tired and hungry, he could hardly walk.

Eventually, he reached a tiny house. In the yard, a lovely young girl was drawing water from a well. 'Hello, there!' Tchang called. She smiled at him, but she did not reply.

An old lady appeared at the door of the house. 'I see you've met my granddaughter, Ai-li,' she called. 'Please don't mind that she didn't greet you. Since the day she was born, she hasn't spoken a word. It makes me very sad.'

• *Ai-li:* (say) 'eye-lee'.

Then she looked closely at Tchang. 'You look worn out! Come inside and have a bite to eat.'

That evening Tchang sat by the fire. He told the pair that he was on his way to ask the Great Wizard of the West a question.

'Good for you!' cried the old woman. 'While you're there, could you ask him why Ai-li can't talk?'

The next day, Tchang set off once again towards the West.

Another forty-nine days passed. The food the old lady gave him soon ran out. Finally, he saw a little hut in the middle of an orchard that was scorched brown by the sun. The land looked so dry and poor, it reminded him of home. An old man appeared in the doorway of the hut. 'Boy!' he called. 'You look worn out! Come inside and rest.'

Later, Tchang told the old man where he was going. 'You're a good boy to undertake such a difficult journey,' said the old man. 'By the way, when you see the Wizard, would you mind asking him why my lemon tree won't bear fruit?'

Tchang agreed, of course.

Next morning, he rose early and set off once more for the West. After yet another forty-nine days he came to a river, fast and deep and wide. His heart sank. There was no way he could cross it.

Suddenly, a great green dragon rose from the water. Even to Tchang, who had never met a dragon before, its tiny wings seemed too small for its body. Set in its forehead was a gorgeous pearl.

Tchang was about to run away, but the dragon called to him. 'Don't be frightened! I'm quite harmless. Tell me why you want to cross my river.'

Tchang explained that he needed to ask the Great Wizard of the West some important questions.

When the Pearl Dragon heard the questions, it smiled. 'You're a good lad, Tchang,' it said. 'Hop on my back and I'll have you across in a jiffy.'

On the far side of the river, Tchang thanked the dragon.

'Think nothing of it!' the dragon replied cheerfully. 'That's what I'm here for. Oh, by the way. While you're there, could you please ask the Wizard why I can't fly? Every dragon in China can fly – except me.'

Naturally, Tchang said yes. He set off again towards the West with the four questions going around and around in his head.

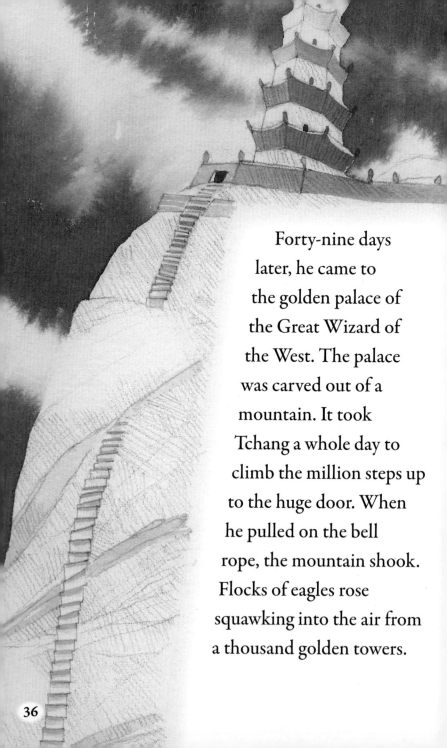

Forty-nine days later, he came to the golden palace of the Great Wizard of the West. The palace was carved out of a mountain. It took Tchang a whole day to climb the million steps up to the huge door. When he pulled on the bell rope, the mountain shook. Flocks of eagles rose squawking into the air from a thousand golden towers.

Chapter 3

The great doors of the palace swung open.
Tchang found himself in a mighty hall. It was
so high he couldn't see the ceiling for clouds.
On a throne at the end of the hall sat the Great
Wizard. He glared down at Tchang. 'Well?' he
bellowed. 'What do you want, boy?'

Tchang tried to stop shaking. 'I ... I have four
questions to ask you, sir!'

'HAH!' shouted the Wizard. 'Then you may
as well go home right now! I will only answer
THREE questions. If you ask me four, I won't
answer any of them. So there!'

Tchang thought his legs would fold underneath him. What could he do? There was his poor mother's question, then the old woman's question, then the old man's question, and then the Pearl Dragon's question. For his own sake, as well as his mother's, he desperately wanted to know the answer to the first question - but he also knew he couldn't let his friends down. So he answered sadly, 'Then I will only ask you three.'

When Tchang had asked his questions a thunderstorm began to rage high up in the hall. The Wizard hurled three scrolls down to Tchang. 'Here are your answers, boy. Now go home!'

Tchang fled from the palace. He leaped down the million stone steps, five at a time.

When he reached the river, the Pearl Dragon was waiting for him. 'Well?' it said. 'What did the Wizard say?'

Tchang opened the scroll marked 'Dragon'. 'He says, if you do something really kind and generous, you'll be able to fly like other dragons.'

'Hmm,' said the Dragon. 'Well, hop aboard and I'll take you across the river.'

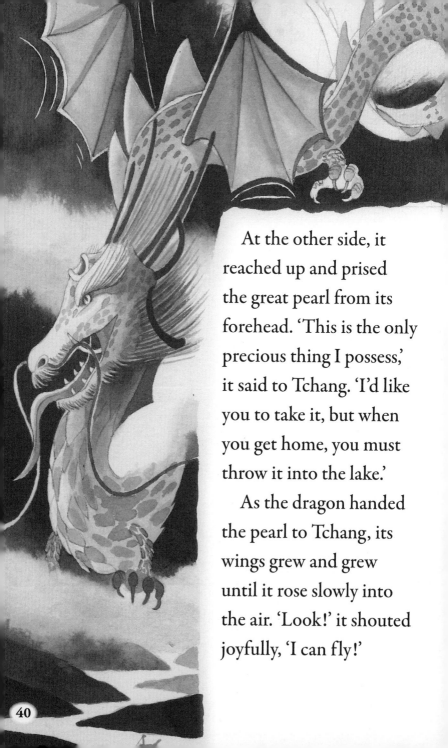

At the other side, it reached up and prised the great pearl from its forehead. 'This is the only precious thing I possess,' it said to Tchang. 'I'd like you to take it, but when you get home, you must throw it into the lake.'

As the dragon handed the pearl to Tchang, its wings grew and grew until it rose slowly into the air. 'Look!' it shouted joyfully, 'I can fly!'

It was winter, now, and snow lay thick upon the land. Tchang struggled on towards the East until he reached the old man's hut.

The old man was delighted to see him. 'So? What did the Wizard say?'

Tchang opened the scroll marked 'Old Man'. 'He says you must look beneath the lemon tree.'

Together they dug at the frozen earth around the tree until they came upon nine golden jars. Water poured from them, as clear as crystal. As it sank into the ground, all the trees in the orchard burst into flower.

The old man was so grateful he gave Tchang one of the golden jars.

Tchang travelled on until he reached the little house in the forest. Ai-li was away tending the sheep. The old woman said, 'So why can't Ai-li speak?'

Tchang opened the scroll marked 'Old Woman'. He replied, 'She will speak when she loves someone with all her heart.'

Then the door opened and there stood Ai-li. 'Tchang!' she cried.

The old woman was overjoyed. She told Tchang, 'You should marry my granddaughter. She will make you a wonderful wife.'

So Tchang and Ai-li were married.

Then they set off again towards the East. Eventually, they reached Tchang's home. His mother didn't see them coming – she had cried for so long, she had gone blind.

Tchang's heart was heavy. How would he tell her that he hadn't even asked the Wizard her question? Then he remembered the pearl. As he took it from his pocket, the light from the pearl shone into his mother's eyes and suddenly she could see again.

Remembering what the dragon had told him, Tchang ran to the lake. He threw the pearl into its deep blue waters. The lake seemed to shudder and heave. Then Tchang saw that it was teeming with fine, fat fish that jumped right out of the water onto the shore.

Tchang unpacked the golden jar. The crystal clear water poured out onto the garden and a forest of flowers sprang from the earth.

Their troubles were finally over. Tchang lived
with his mother and Ai-li and their children
for many long and happy years. And every day,
the Pearl Dragon would soar high overhead
and smile down upon them.

The Bamburgh Dragon

A legend from Northumbria, England

Chapter 1

A great rambling castle stands beside the wild sand dunes on the coast of Northumbria.

Long ago, a king lived there with his daughter Margaret and his son Prince Wynde. One misty morning the King and Margaret waved farewell to Prince Wynde. He was setting out to sea, alone. The sea was dark and restless. Lightning flickered on the horizon.

The boat vanished into the gloom. The King and Margaret sadly made their way indoors.

They didn't notice the fat, grinning toad by the castle gates. It was watching their every move with its bulging glassy eyes.

- *Bamburgh:* (say) 'bam-bruh'.
- *Wynde:* (say) 'wind' (rhymes with 'kind').

That night, a terrible storm blew up.
The King and his daughter were beside
themselves with worry for Prince Wynde.

The tempest raged for seven days. Margaret
tried to keep the King busy. They played
draughts and chess while the wind howled
around the towers, rattling the windows and
shaking the walls.

The eighth day dawned still and bright. The sea
lapped at the shore as if nothing had happened.

Then someone rang the great brass bell.

'Your Highness,' announced a servant. 'A lady
wishes to speak with you. She says she has news
of the Prince.'

The King leapt from his throne and strode across his chamber. 'Bring her to me at once!' he cried.

The woman was uncommonly beautiful. She had long hair, as black as night, and dark, bewitching eyes.

The King's heart was pounding for fear of what she might tell him. But the woman smiled. She told him, in a sweet, musical voice, that Prince Wynde had sailed to an island haven when the storm broke. He was safe and well.

The King nearly fainted with relief. His heart still pounded but for a different reason – he had fallen hopelessly in love with this dark stranger.

Margaret was alarmed. There was something very odd about their visitor. How did she know her brother was safe? Why was her father so besotted with her? It was only a few months since her dear mother, the Queen, had passed away.

The King bade the servants prepare the best room in the castle for his guest. He invited her to stay for supper. The meal did nothing to ease Margaret's fears. There was something inhuman about the woman, however beautiful she might seem. She reminded Margaret of a reptile.

Next day, the woman showed no sign of leaving. In fact, she had no intention of leaving at all. Not that the King minded: he seemed more and more enchanted by her every day.

Finally, Margaret took him aside. 'Father, what's come over you? That woman has put you under some sort of spell!'

'How dare you talk to me like that?' shouted the King. 'She is a good, kind person. In fact, I intend to marry her.'

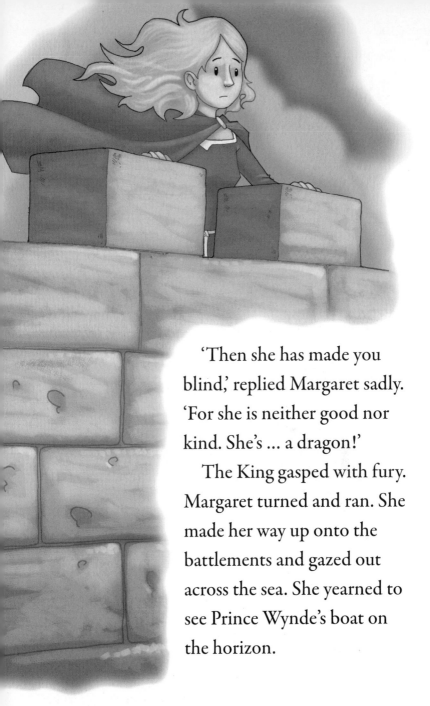

'Then she has made you blind,' replied Margaret sadly. 'For she is neither good nor kind. She's ... a dragon!'

The King gasped with fury. Margaret turned and ran. She made her way up onto the battlements and gazed out across the sea. She yearned to see Prince Wynde's boat on the horizon.

The stranger had heard every word. In no time at all she appeared before Margaret, her black eyes blazing. 'Ever since I arrived,' she cried, 'you have tried to turn the King against me. You're jealous. You can't stand him paying me any attention. You princesses are all the same!'

'My father is a lonely old man,' replied Margaret quietly. 'I wish above all else that he would find someone to cherish and care for him. But you are not that someone. You have bewitched him.'

'Hah!' shrieked the enchantress. 'That
does it! You called me a dragon. Now we'll
see who the dragon is!' She raised her hands
above her head and muttered some words in a
harsh, unknown tongue. There was a blinding
flash and Margaret was turned into a raging,
snarling, bellowing ... DRAGON.

The beautiful stranger threw back her
head and let out a horrible
screeching laugh.
It was neither
sweet nor musical.
It shattered the
windows in the castle.

The dragon lashed its tail, snapping the flagpole like a matchstick. It breathed a great cloud of smoke and fire that, but for her magical powers, would have fried the enchantress. It struck the battlements with its wicked claws, sending heavy chunks of stone crashing down into the castle moat.

'Temper, temper, Margaret!' cried the witch – for witch she most surely was. 'Daddy won't like you wrecking the place!'

The dragon lunged at her with a deafening roar, but she ducked into a doorway and disappeared.

Chapter 2

Far out to sea, a small boat drifted on the windless water. The Prince sat in the stern, enjoying the warm evening breeze and the sunset. He was glad to be alive. The storm had nearly sunk his boat. Luckily, he had found shelter on an island and waited for the waves to die down.

He yawned, he stretched – and then he froze. For on the horizon, exactly where his father's castle stood, a great ball of fire rose into the air. 'The castle's burning!' he cried. He snatched up his oars and began to row as fast as he could.

Meanwhile, under the witch's evil spell, the dragon rampaged through the castle. It smashed furniture. It scorched the ancient tapestries that covered the walls. The servants cowered in the cellar while the King hid, trembling, under his four-poster bed.

The dragon was mad with hunger. It blundered into the kitchen and set about eating everything in it – whole sides of beef and baskets of vegetables. It even ate the fire irons and the blazing logs in the fireplace.

Prince Wynde dragged his boat up the beach. Smoke was pouring from the kitchen windows as he raced across the drawbridge. 'Father? Margaret?' he shouted. There was no reply.

He made straight for the kitchen, grabbing a bucket of water on the way.

A few seconds later the bucket clattered onto the kitchen floor. The Prince was stunned to find himself facing not a fire, but a huge, angry, fire-breathing dragon.

'Welcome home, Prince Wynde!' called a mocking voice behind him. He turned to see a beautiful stranger. 'Say hello to your little sister! My, hasn't she grown?'

'Margaret?' he cried, gazing at the unhappy creature. The dragon stopped its roaring and stared back at him with huge sad eyes.

Now the Prince was no fool. He realised the stranger was really a witch. He had to act and act quickly! He dimly remembered that the way to break a witch's spell was to kiss her. He took a deep breath and winked at the dragon.

Then he turned to the woman, smiling his most charming smile. He fell on one knee and took her hand. 'Madam, such beauty! Pray grant me a kiss?'

The witch looked at him, surprised. But she was vain. So vain that she could not say no. 'Oh, go on then!' she purred.

Prince Wynde sprang to his feet, seized her in his arms and kissed her. Then, very quickly, two things happened.

One: the beautiful enchantress began to melt in his arms. She wriggled and shrank and gurgled and squeaked until she turned into a fat, loathsome toad. She dropped to the floor with a plop!

Two: the dragon exploded. There was a fearsome crack and a cloud of smoke. All that remained of the dragon was its heart. With a horrible, soggy, ripping sound, it split in two – and out stepped Margaret.

Later, at the dinner table, the King raised
a glass to his two children. 'Thank you both.
I hope you will forgive a foolish old man for
falling in love with a beautiful enchantress.'

'Don't worry, Father,' said Margaret. 'It
happens all the time. Beautiful enchantresses
can be a real nuisance!'

Margaret's words floated through the air
to where a fat toad crouched outside the
castle walls.

To this very day, visitors to Bamburgh Castle rarely notice the toad that watches their every move through bulging, glassy eyes.